This book is dedicated to all of the babies born in the Permian Basin. You are our future students, workforce, and community members.

www.mascotbooks.com

For more information, please contact:
Mascot Books
620 Herndon Parkway, Suite 320
Herndon, VA 20170
info@mascotbooks.com

Library of Congress Control Number: 2020902320

CPSIA Code: PRFRE0420A
ISBN-13: 978-1-64543-422-1

Printed in Canada

O is for Oil
The ABCs of Odessa

ADRIAN VEGA

Illustrated by Agus Prajogo

Aa is for **A**rmadillos roaming the West Texas highways.

Bb
is for Basins filled with oil.

Cc is for Cactus in the fields.

Dd is for Drill sites dotted across the land.

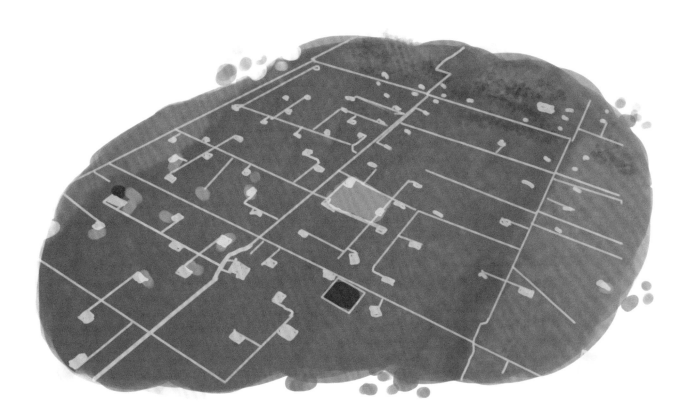

Ee is for the Ellen Noël Art Museum.

Ff is for Fiesta West Texas.

Gg is for the Globe Theatre at Odessa College.

Hh

is for Hot Summer Nights concerts downtown.

Ii is for Ice skating at Music City Mall.

Jj

is for the Odessa Jackalopes.

 **is for Keep Odessa Beautiful.**

 is for the Parade of **L**ights
in downtown Odessa.

Mm

is for the Odessa **M**arriott
and Conference Center.

Nn is for the Night sky in West Texas.

Oo is for Oil in Odessa.

Pp
is for Pipelines
flowing with oil.

Qq is for West Texas Quail.

Rr

is for Jack Ben Rabbit, Odessa's official mascot.

Ss is for Stonehenge at the University of Texas Permian Basin.

Tt is for Traffic boxes as public art throughout the city.

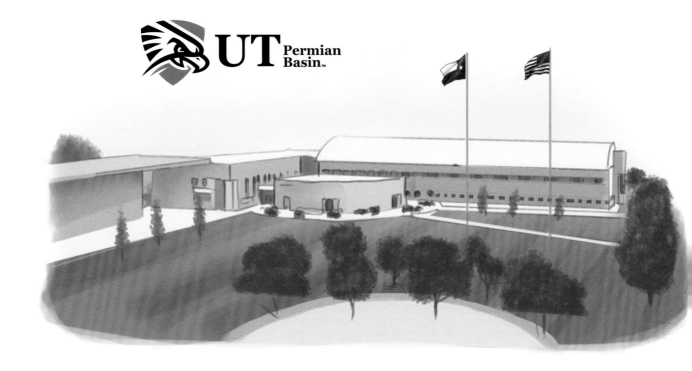

Uu is for The University of Texas Permian Basin.

Vv

is for Starbright Village at McKinney Park in December.

Ww is for the Wranglers of Odessa College.

 is for XTO Energy, helping fuel West Texas and beyond.

Yy
is for Red Yucca growing tall.

Zz is for Zumba classes offered throughout the city.

About the Author

Adrian Vega is a former public school educator of 20 years. He began his public education career as a 2nd grade teacher and still has a vested interest in childhood education despite no longer being in the classroom. In addition to penning *O is for Oil*, Adrian is also the creator and author of *The Adventures of El Super Lector* series, which features a bilingual, biliterate superhero who promotes literacy. Adrian is married to Kathryn, and they have two children: Avery and Della.

The Power of Words and Early Reading (POWER) is a community-based initiative that focuses on the promotion of language development and early literacy in the Permian Basin. As part of an Education Partnership of the Permian Basin, early childhood initiative, POWER's purpose is to encourage the community to read, speak, and interact with children as frequently as possible, beginning at birth. The mission of POWER is to provide the community with tools and resources to help promote language development and early literacy in children, beginning at birth. While the vision of POWER is that all children in the Permian Basin enter school kindergarten-ready.

100 percent of the Education Partnership's proceeds from *O is for Oil: The ABCs of Odessa* will go to support the POWER Bag initiative in the Permian Basin.

POWER Bags are provided to every mother who gives birth at Medical Center Hospital (MCH) and Odessa Regional Medical Center (ORMC) upon discharge from the hospital. As part of the POWER Bag initiative, medical staff at each hospital provide mothers with information about brain development, language development, and the importance of speaking, interacting, and reading to their newborn. **www.powerbag.org**

The Education Partnership of the Permian Basin would like to offer a special word of thanks to the Odessa Marriott and XTO Energy. Their generous contribution to the POWER Bag initiative made it possible for *O is for Oil: The ABCs of Odessa* to be published and to be placed in each POWER Bag.